T0007135

ORION SWEEPING

Library and Archives Canada Cataloguing in Publication

Title: Orion sweeping / Anne Marie Todkill.
Names: Todkill, Anne Marie, author.
Description: Poems.
Identifiers: Canadiana (print) 20210320931 | Canadiana (ebook) 2021032581x |
ISBN 9781771315692 (softcover) | ISBN 9781771315708 (HTML) |
ISBN 9781771315715 (PDF)
Classification: LCC PS8639.O355 O75 2022 | DDC C811/.6—dc23

Copyright © Anne Marie Todkill, 2022

We acknowledge the Canada Council for the Arts, the Government of Canada
through the Canada Book Fund, and the Ontario Arts Council for their support
of our publishing program.

 Canada Council   Conseil des arts
for the Arts   du Canada   Canadä   ONTARIO ARTS COUNCIL
CONSEIL DES ARTS DE L'ONTARIO

The author photo was taken by Lawrence Wardroper.
The book is set in Fournier and Filson Pro.
Designed by Marijke Friesen.
Cover image by ArtBalitskiy.
Edited by Barry Dempster.
Printed and bound by Coach House Printing.

Brick Books
487 King St. W.
Kingston, ON
K7L 2X7
www.brickbooks.ca

Though much of the work of Brick Books takes place on the ancestral lands of the
Anishinaabeg, Haudenosaunee, Huron-Wendat, and Mississaugas of the Credit
peoples, our editors, authors, and readers from many backgrounds are situated
from coast to coast to coast in Canada on the traditional and unceded territories of
over six hundred nations who have cared for Turtle Island from time immemorial.
While living and working on these lands, we are committed to hearing and return-
ing the rightful imaginative space to the poetries, songs, and stories that have been
untold, under-told, wrongly told, and suppressed through colonization.

In memoriam PJT

EARTH

Strontium-90

Campaigning for peace,
their mothers gathered teeth:
too big for fairies now,
but we can show the President
how wrong a thing is war,
how poisonous the test bombs
blooming in deserts blowing closer.
What use, the baby/milk/deciduous teeth,
once shed as easily as leaves or tears,
unless to mail proof that death's particulates
have fallen on pastures, are rising like sap
in the tender limbs of children.

How sensibly the mothers of St. Louis
washed, dried, and sealed these tokens of belief
(whiff of blood, perhaps bacteria); and
thinking how quickly time gathers into years
(indulging, no doubt, in some relief:
all done, the hot-cheeked days of teething,
bitter discipline of weaning) wrote intimate truths
on the survey cards (months on breast,
on formula, where born, where in utero)
while their gap-gummed warriors, still shocked
by the tug when the worried root released,
tongued the small craters, noted the metal taste,
and pinned on their badges: *I gave my tooth to science.*

Trinitite

The desert,
enraptured,
seeded the cloud
with glass.

Up it went.
Up it went.
Earth-bound man
leaped from the ground.

And what fell out
was trinket, trophy,
doublethink,
mineral babble, bauble,
afterbirth. Bottle green,
unless occluded
with traces of the tower,
copper wire, or the device.
Less radioactive
than you'd imagine:
less, for example,
than a smoke detector
or two hundred ripe bananas.

The *sons of bitches*
posed there later,
in the *lake of jade*,

a shallow bowl
of civilization.

At Valles Caldera
we stared for ages
at tiny specks
in the grassy plain
until we realized
they were cattle grazing
on the blistered earth.

The public staircase in Toronto now named the Baldwin Steps

Looking back
made the climb add up
to something, like fact
or revelation: the world
worlding as CN needle,
reimagined lakefront,
Lego-mapled blocks laid out
with the fabulous detail
of anonymity.
Below the escarpment
a dairy fleet hummed,
ready for the night run
from a sticky city
with a sweet tooth.

(pigeon, staggering
on a hot-mopped roof)

Any vantage is enough
to reposition history:
some hold it close
as a stone's throw,
a Tonka-toy catastrophe

(asphalt miasma
rising like thirst)

and it may be true
that fear of heights
has less to do with falling
than the making-strange of scale,
unless it's just the raising
of possibility that tilts you
off-plane, like Van Gogh's chair,
precarious in the third dimension.

(chain link pinned
to the faulted earth)

I couldn't tell you now
what I was leaving or going to
up the zigzag of those stairs
or what, if anything, we called them.

The risen land.
Ishpadinaa.

(the bird-shot sky
releasing starlings)

Route options

A prayer to St. Christopher.

Avoid ferries.
Avoid tolls.
Avoid highways,
meaning roads
without landedness,
not places but vectors,
all forwardness,
unmemoried,
bodiless.

Saint of the stilt legs;
you, of the lucky medallions
and shatterproof figurines;
you, the Ungainly, who waded
the heavy Child across a torrent;
you, whom I have glimpsed in passing,
high-bellied above water
as great blue heron and, once,
a moose, guardian of steadiness:
save me from peril.

From level crossings, sink holes,
iced bridges, drifting snow,
shredded rubber, stray stones,
crumbled shoulders, rumble strips,

collectors, slips, cross-lane merges,
the vacuum suck of transports
with hubcaps spiked like chariots',
and shadow deer
rising from ditches,
deliver me.

Let me not be hypnotized
by cat's-eyes on night asphalt.

Shield me from rages,
fast-food oases,
and all forms of morbid haste
on the 400 series of highways.

Hide from me the flare
of roadside crosses'
unfading flowers.

Grant me patience,
overburdened saint,
to etch-a-sketch west,
now south, now west,
now south, my halting traverse;
let me not outpace
all-terrains dusting up railbeds
to folly mines, vanished pines;
post limits safe for rumination
on the flash of lakes, trace

of colonizing lines, scars
of settlement and heartbreak,
the tramp of picketmen
and chainbearers, and my forebear's
zealous ghost, still figuring the azimuth,
the only of his crew to drown
when you abandoned them
crossing Balsam Lake.

Oh, saint.

Let me not lament
barns skeletal or sinking,
machines that scrape
the sediment of ages
from drumlins west of Madoc,
pine plantations on oak moraines,
rolling fields of ethanol,
reptile zoos, dinosaur farms,
powdery alpacas in the first skiff of snow,
wedding-dress shops at the crossroads of nowhere,
scrap-metal yards, car-dealer rows,
the rising tideline of razed concessions,
mansions squatting on severances
behind faux castle gates with views
down the watershed to Lake Ontario,
the boundless city a reversed Elysium.

Ask me not what the present means,
its signs and remonstrations:
No turbines without science.
Stop sprawl.
Slow down.
Pray for the persecuted Church.
Hot-tub liquidators.
Pick your own rapini.
Please, no engine brakes.

Sure-footed saint,
grant thy blessing
to travellers like me,
born not to the wrong century
but at the wrong speed.

Let me take
let me take
let me take the slow road
let me take the road slow.

Trove

That might have been
a beetle glinting
like old bronze
in the split earth.
Maybe it was just
water slicking the clay,
a flake of mica,
scrap of cellophane
glimpsed too late
between spade-strokes.
It's earthed again now,
an incidental finding
in the bean patch
where I set rows of seeds
as white as grubs.
They will shoulder through
the ground after rain,
arching pale stems,
dragging their cotyledons,
startled, into daylight.

Trace

When the March sun, warming,
opens tracks, as if all beasts
who passed this way were giant—
the fox, coyote; coyote, wolf;
the wolf (if such it was)
measuring up to myth—
I feel a mild ambivalence.
Relief, that earth at last
is leaning in our favour
toward spring; regret, at the loss
of evidence. Some canid or other
came this way (as if nature feasts
on generalities). If you think
my craving for precision
is a merely human thing,
tell that to the fisher
who followed through winter's
long crepuscule the porcupine's
furrowed path and left
a scrap of belly fur,
fan of quills,
dark fragments drawing heat
to the softening earth.

Teachings of the mink

Be nimble, said the mink.
Don't linger: look quick
for glint of fish.
Dip now, whip your
half-webbed feet.
Pierce crisp scales.
Grip fast the silver
muscle. Rise then,
feast.

Be supple, said the mink.
Flow under ice.
Melt into stone.
Be river-dark, cryptic.

Dazzle, said the mink.
Sit tall, shining, slick.
Cast pearls at winter's feet.
Hold your white chin
raised, alert.
Mesmerize watchers.
They will not know
your oil-bright eyes
are weak.

Prepare for famine,
said the mink.
Break empty shells;
sharpen teeth.
Save scraps.
Be silent.
Sneak.

Prosper, said the mink,
by stealth and murder.
Take muskrats
in their mounds,
voles breathing
under snow.
Drag them, steaming;
gorge; drink deep.
Curl round
the belly-fire
of the kill.
Longbody, rest.
Save heat.

Follow, said the mink,
my flourishes on snow.
As water stains paper
I mark your thoughts
fleetly
as the shadow of a crow.

Sighting

Crossing the beach road, a stick animal
with long legs, straight back, prick ears,
dusty coat flat in the sunshine, moves
at a slow trot, turns its head toward us,
suspends its gait for an instant before
slipping into the trees, caught on the retina
like a memory more than anything.

Coyote is the name we retrieve: *Look, a coyote.*
They're extending their range here, shape-shifting
with Algonquin wolves, the bloodlines uncertain.
We've seen their traces in the morning on the track
above the lake, the pillaged cache of turtle eggs,
shells furled in the sand like pale magnolias.

But if this dog is, on the other hand, a wolf
then it was a wolf we saw that time
near Deception Lake, remember?
(We always meant to ask about the name.)
It was the same apparition on a dry road,
looking at us sideways, dusky-grey and lean,
taking the measure of our doubt,
then vanishing.

Toward a definition of wildness

The fox before you saw it.
The fox before it saw you.
The fox before it knew it had been seen.
You, before you had thought of the fox.
You in the moment of seeing, when you were all fox.

Thirst

As soon as we arrive the dog forges her direction,
and we are impressed by the precision of her desire,
the clarity of her escape where the path forks
between human encampments (Coleman stoves,
collapsible chairs) and the way to the boat launch.
She shames us with our mistake: the car-weary dog
needs water and, naturally, smells the lake, the glacial sink
where, since the retreat, have settled the molecules
of crustaceans, charophytes, intoxicating gases of decay—
this lake which, as if noseless, we will call crystalline
when we peer over the gunwale of a rented canoe,
practise handstands at the beach, and note the glint of mica
in the shallows when the sun warms the rocky bays
like so many bathtubs in late afternoon
and even the minnows are languid. But later,
in the tent, after our paddle, our swim,
the drenchings of her mighty shake, we will taste it on skin:
the salts of ages, tang of unknown proteins, acids, alkalis,
photodermal reactions, modern lotions of prevention;
and rocking on imprinted waves settle into sleep,
where our dreams will be of perils (waterfalls, deserts,
difficult births) until we wake to her panting,
the static of cicadas, and know by our thirst
that we are little more than water,
rising to air, draining to earth.

Farmyard behaviour

The young boar, sleek and undersized,
mounted the sow he barely had
the height for with little preamble
and no fuss while she stood, unsurprised—
the pair almost motionless, undramatic,
as if this were merely a way of one leaning
on the other in repose. This repeats,
the farmer said, several times a day,
whenever the boar remembers the sow
and opportunity are there: *Oh, right, you.*
A pig's penis is corkscrewed, like the tail,
she explained, but we never caught a glimpse
and slid past the placid couple into the barn
to see how things had worked out
with an ingenious storage room for grain,
a bumper crop this year, oats and barley
grown together in one field.

AIR

Remex

Flight feather, from the Latin remus, *oar.*

1

I once mistook for hawk
a barred quill found on our road
like a signature of wildness,
but then recalled
the phony restoration
in these townships
of turkeys to be shot.
Of all the absent birds,
why salvage this, not only
beyond its range but ludicrous?
Give me a bobolink, for God's sake,
give me a pair of meadowlarks.
But a feather's a feather,
so I swished it (as one does),
testing for the angles that prove
the density of air, and I have to say
the kick on the downstroke
was tremendous. With enough
of these glued to my arms
I could be that turkey, Icarus.

2

Working in pairs, dihedral,
rocking on the vertex,
vultures wheel the clearing,

inflecting arc and altitude
with the tilt of an oar blade
as easily as you or I might lift
a finger, change the subject,
release a breath. Pilots
at the height of indolence;
they expend more energy
standing on the ground,
which may be why
their terrible descent
is rare if not reluctant,
the darkening wings
like the kurogo
of a shaded puppeteer,
serenely enfolding
his character in death.

Central Experimental Farm, April

1
Open your hand,
drop a flat stone
into reedy water,
watch it fall
through the fret;
note the slight wobble,
weird slo-mo,
like a memory
of how to float.

Wild geese
sink into fields like that,
reassessing weightlessness,
rocking earthward
in a sling of air.

2
They have our number
and keep dialing it at night,
at daybreak, beeping us awake
the way the sound of local traffic
penetrates, the recycling truck's
rear-wheel brakes, the restlessness
of all things normal and recurrent.

3

The snowfall's been thin,
near-record low, as if winter
(was it boredom? incompetence?)
was secònded to some other season.
We've had no stockpile,
no windrow drifts,
no frozen assets waiting for release,
and now (most bitterly) no thaw:
just this freezer burn,
high-pressure stall,
stingy sublimation,
parching last year's
harrow-work to stone,
leaving lichen scabs
of salt-grit on the roads,
ice polished under tires
to onyx cabochons.

4

The ugly earth.
Pig-iron fields.
Someone tell the geese
they've come too early.
This isn't spring,
but west along Baseline
a superstore garden
has potted it
under awnings.

5

Pity the epic geese,
skidding into gravity,
awkward with their landing gear down
and the autopilot malfunctioning.
It takes an effort: not just wing-baffle
brakes them, but all that migratory muscle.
Look at them, twelve-pound honkers
hanging onto air like an old belief.

6

We put ourselves up there,
watching the throb
of their imperfect chevrons
(eternal realignment,
fracture, and repair),
worried by the sense they give
of our own weariness.
But when we watch
the night flights landing,
their ponderous hover
above hard fields,
it's the coming-to-earth,
the tragicomical surrender,
that chastens us.

7

Who can tell whether
that glass-bead gaze
is gormless or self-aware;
the implied pince-nez,
paratrooper chin-cup.
All long-necked birds
pose as caricatures.
We might say this:
geese resting in the stubble
of demonstration corn
are in every way exemplary.
They signify themselves,
the solace of return,
our satisfaction with such things
and, hence, ourselves.
The geese are back.
Obvious, that it does us good
to see them.
They are as we are,
tautologous with time.
Heideggerian, these geese,
Colvillesque, silver edged,
monumental and ordinary,
a sacred and pragmatic flock,
finding God knows what
in frost-scaled fields
tender or sufficient to eat.

Yard duty

When I release my puppy
on a gang of winter crows
it is not because I hate them
or believe they're less entitled
than the finches I mean to feed,
but only to admire
how athletically she springs
and never catches
the blue light flashing
from their wings.

Chickadee

Tame feeder, your
small grip tense
as a bonsai root,
do you despise
this urge I have
to close my hand
and hold you
for a moment still?

November, Stormont County

1

Hawk month. Glint-light slant,
clouds smudged mauve. Fields
like salt prints, tarnished. Corn
sere or stubbled. Brush-piles
flaring vermilion; smoke stretching
leeward, low. Backhoes paused
beside trenched earth, black spools
of drainage pipe. In the distance,
as if silent, a train from Montreal.

2

Keep one eye on traffic, the other
on roadside trees, until you see
a bleb in dry branches that is not
an empty hive of paper wasps,
squirrel pod, curled porcupine,
or plastic bag snagged by wind,
but a red-tail hunkered above ditches,
waiting for a signal: vole.
Voler.
You'll never match that readiness.
In a moment you'll mistake
five hundred buntings landing
for a skiff of snow.

3

Ex nihilo, through silver air: flecks,
floaters, filaments, then strands, braids,
squalls of snow geese, powdering
the cornfield, sewage lagoon, shaved field,
landfill, any fuel stop on the flyway,
flashing their insignia (black on the wing tip,
very sharp), signalling likeness, signalling kind,
stirring unrest, the usual brawls, wind-rush
of babble, rousing the night flyers, who lift,
swirl, settle, lift, heliographing *now, now,*
and *almost, almost,* flagging traffic into lines,
chromosome crossings, x and y, breaking
and repairing until the glyph appears,
aerodynamic letterform for *follow, follow,*
while each bird, rising, thins to a cypher,
wing-belly-wing, black-white-black marker,
shimmering particle, code.

Flight delay with telephoto

Stranger to me
than the ravening bird
was the woman with a stroller
who just kept walking
while I stood as plainly
as a cartoon paparazza
behind a scrawny tree.
So I pointed to the incident
in progress by the curb:
Cooper's hawk, eating pigeon.

Wide-eyed, she hovered
(the woman, I mean)
above a tricky landing spot
between beauty and indecency
(and what kind of weirdo
did she make of me,
with my ghoulish lens
and hobby documentary?)
but glancing toward
the sleeping child
we naturally agreed:
lucky the baby can't see
this quasi-cannibal
strewing feathers on the grass
as remorselessly as a farm cook

on the stoop of her summer kitchen
stripping a chicken for the pot,
the flurry of down
weightless and derisory.

These murders are common
in this end of town. And now
I've got this hawk's MO:
tweezing grey quills
(the knowledge intimate,
from preening),
tossing soft semiplumes
(a few settled like epaulettes),
pulling pale strings of meat
(they hung carelessly from her beak),
swivelling her gaze for competitors
(the agate eye gorgeous).

What I didn't expect
were the baggage checks,
testing liftoff with the carcass
pinned so deeply you'd think
she'd jessed herself.
Almost overkill,
only a female, mature,
would attempt it.

I didn't notice
when my neighbour left.
But I wish she could see
how certain frames
viewed in high-res
show the pale rufous
on culottes and breast
as elastic lines
of sharply drawn arrows,
tessellated
like houndstooth
on white fabric

or Escher's flying birds
eternally trading
figure and ground,
completing the sky
with perfect multiples
of reversal.

Flock

1

The crow-current, ragged river, that flows
above our houses in the closing down of winter
afternoons, pouring in from open fields
outside the city to the south, has been shoaling
here for some reason, pooling on roofs
and the bare canopies of condemned ash trees
on our street. Thousands of them, honestly
tens of thousands, have been streaming over
in recent years, landing in parking lots,
congregating in Coronation Park and
the stand of trees behind the veterans' hospital.
But not in this neighbourhood so much.
So you have to wonder why it didn't happen
before, this sudden debouchment,
why they never crowded here but kept on going
north and east, and what's so different now—
unless with their swollen numbers
(who can account for it?) their roosts
got too rowdy and sleepless, even for crows.

2

I saw a woman in slippers on her driveway
squawking for them to take the party somewhere else.
And although I've taken pleasure
in provoking crows, making them scatter,

stirring them up, I wished she would stop.
I find their silhouettes apt against a smoky sky,
provocateurs lurking in trench coats,
coolly dropping shitballs on our cars.
In the woodlot where we walk the dogs
the smell of ammonia has turned us back—
but who doesn't like the cawing,
the swagger, the flash-mob readiness,
the virtuoso nonchalance.

Hitchcock hour, a neighbour calls it,
but let's stick to the facts and say
crow time, since they know no hour—
only the retracting light, the cooling wind
that chivvies them here with a beauty
not unlike the shreds of garbage bags
fluttering over the landfill near Carp.

3
Have you seen them? I said to the skinny guy
at the dog park, pointing over his shoulder
to the sky. All he could muster was *Whoa*,
the latter-day vowel shift for *wow*, for *hold
the phone*, for *I have never seen so many
freaking crows*. (*Whoa* was once for horses,
like the bright bay who skittered from the lunge line
before I'd clipped it on; that one ignored my *whoa*,
my *easy now*, my *waa-aalk*, but went along with

teerr-rrott, since that's what he was doing anyhow,
and settled his live-wire step into a circle
of habit as if he'd lost the knack for instinct.)

They do this every evening at this hour,
I explained to the young man with the possibly
illegal terrier, and I sensed him orbiting back
from fear into a revised logic of the normal.
That's impressive, he finally replied,
a phrase so precise and ordinary
that despite our differences (age, gender,
sociolect, dog breed) we gazed up together
calmly as if nature was our own idea.

4
My father, whose winters now are ninety-five
(counting that unsettled Lent, last of the Great War,
when the doctor risked his motorcar in a storm),
keeps wanting to know have I put enough seed out
to keep our visitors satisfied. So I tell him
the city flock's a hundred thousand or more,
and we can't have the whole mob at our door.
The trouble is, those crows are the only birds
big enough for him to recognize. He takes it
personally, their bold assemblies in our yard,
pools of them spreading like black oil on snow,
scarfing spillage from a hopper filled for redpolls.
Look at the size of them, my father says,

and it's taken me ages to understand: he thinks
we owe them more. *If I had the energy,* he says,
I'd set up a platform and fill it with corn, and I imagine him
planning how to build it, what fittings he'd salvage
to attach it to a pole, and how he'd be hoping
for an early thaw (the orchards stood in mud
the week after he was born) to plant it deep enough
to hold the weight of a hundred crows.

FAMILIA

Orion sweeping

Approaching midnight,
you on a ladder
planted in the berm
that slumped from the solar panels
before rain and graupel
made this sticky amalgam
that will foil our clever plan
for photon capture
after days of snow,
our batteries and comfort
running down.
So I brace the ladder
at this crazy hour
while you get the job done,
preparing for sunrise
on the second longest
night of the year.

The array rears
against the blueprint sky
like the wings of a satellite,
gargantuan contraption
for phoning home,
while you, apologizing,
send avalanches down,
plastering me, stuccoing the dog,

who shrugs off her surprise
with the usual equanimity
(she loves the cold, the night,
the trace of mice on the ground).

I take my chances,
scanning the sky
while we plunge at a thousand
klicks per second
toward the Great Attractor
and constellations
dredge the near horizon
of blackened cedars
oh so slowly. There, Orion,
whom some call Winter Maker,
belt and dagger sharp as ice,
pitches back-footed
to load his bow; and you,
Winter Sweeper, thin as a diagram
underneath your duffled
silhouette, aim your push-broom
against the dark, leaning
to the edge of the glass,
swinging, one-footed,
in your orbit,
for the moment
undisturbed
by the reckless earth.

Clearing windthrow from the trail

Striking, how trees
so often fall in pairs
like the long married,
the ground heaving
under one and then
so quickly the other
that it's hard to say
which was propping,
which leaning,
or whether they'd grown
together so closely
that it was all the same.

We slice the boles
with bow saw and
pull saw rather than lug
the new Stihl all this way,
but use the cutting
order we were taught—
compression, then tension—
to avoid pinching the blades.
Even in these soft logs
straddling the path, balsam,
slender, we hear the snap
of the last fibres taking
the remaining weight,
then breaking.

Wash day

After forty-seven years
the laundry tub gave out.
Just like that.
Finally, my mother said,
like she'd been waiting for this day
to dispense her standard line:
Well, nothing lasts forever.
Just think of the uses
for that phrase—infatuations,
lilacs, good ice for skating—
the curiously strong lozenge
she always had ready
to clear our minds of grief.
(Cool as peppermint she was,
the day I left my husband.)
But I'd have to say
that in the family inventory
of things that didn't last,
the double concrete laundry tub
was the most surprising.
It sprang a leak and we said,
It was bound to happen eventually,
as if we really had believed
that such a simple thing could fail.
Those modern detergents, my father said,
*were eating out the wire mesh
all this time.*

The sound was quite a shocker:
metal on stone,
rising from the basement
while they whacked the thing
into pieces.
Clang
                forty-seven years
      clang.

Tough as the dickens,
my father said, resting
the sledgehammer on the floor.
When my mother took it from his hands
he showed her where to land the blows.

Laser correction of posterior capsular opacification subsequent to cataract implant surgery

He gave me the observation deck,
so to speak, the auxiliary lens
of his surgical machine,
as if duty somehow made
a willing student out of me.
Watch now, he whispered—
do you see?

But I saw nothing more distinct
in that dark galaxy than
lost planets, fading stars,
milky nebulae,
fragments of asteroids—
and four red dots
squaring the beam
like beacons marking
a landing strip
on a rainy night.

See it now?
And so I did—
a chasm widening
with each pulse,
the clouded capsule

breaking:
thin ice,
black water.

Exactly, said the wizard
looking up from his glass,
but I knew he didn't see
the way I did
the looming infinity
in the deep starry vitreous
of my father's ancient eye.

Fall risk

1

The way it rests, poised in the wire of pin cherries
below, the *port de bras* convincing, you could be here
until spring before noticing that this is a broken limb,
out of action, a drunken stiff hoisted hand over hand
to the swinging saloon door—only there's no exit here,
nowhere to go but down to good clean dirt.
A lot more's got to give before this carbon starts over,
yields to earth, blooms with fungi. And who knew
those stunted cherries could be so strong, shade-grown
under the garrulous veteran (sugar maple, retired,
so old its cells have slowed past apoptosis to a long,
amnesiac drying), singled out by chance as if planted
in a row for this exact (no matter how haphazard) purpose.

One more storm might bring that branch down.
Then again, trees this old can fracture unprovoked,
like icebergs calving, cliffs flaking into sea,

or my father's brother,
who, rising from the table,
broke, then fell.

2

When the falling starts, we fear our own weight,
covertly brittle bones, take bisphosphonates
to slow our self-dissolving, submit to the walker,
the balance exercises. But there's no remedy
for chance. My uncle was alone, worse luck,
when he shattered to the floor. By the time
he crawled from the kitchen to the phone
he saw how things must be recomposed.
A brave and truthful man, he made it
a clean break, his last night at home.

3

My father, at a vertiginous age, learned
to use a sideways two-step for stairs,
a steady method for rising from chairs,
a telescopic claw to pick up slippers.
Falls are inevitable, the therapists said,
but we do what we can to forestall them.

Sure enough, in the nursing home,
two backward topples, no warning.
He went down like an oak
without splitting.

In the end days they lifted him,
stork-wise, in a sling, a procedure
that bruised him more than anything:
more than the empty-tank landing

on coastal patrol, into the sea;
the front-step stumble that winged him
at eighty; the ninety-something wipeout
in the garage. Hearing the racket,
I opened the door; the bird
he was shooing flew in.

I dusted him off.
He brushed off my scolding.
What the heck, he said.
It was so unexpected.

I caught the dove where it landed
on the kitchen windowsill.

I'm no one to talk. My tally includes
a full-body slam from a gallop
(the clay field was hard but spangled with violets),
a spread-eagled drop from a chairlift
(my father, incredulous, witnessed),
and a nifty flip on a borrowed bike
when the front wheel seized on a hill
(for an instant, my handstand was perfect).

But the one that matters is the ur-fall
of family lore: my father carrying me down
from the room that served as nursery,
wearing sock feet on the hardwood stair.

With each retelling, my mother scolded:
How many times had I told you.

I always thought he was the hero, though,
pulling off a two-stage pratfall to save the baby,
a sacrificial spine-cracker while he hoisted me
at arm's length in the air. Gravity handled him
roughly; judiciously, he took the fall, suspending us
ever after in the strange gift we apparently shared
for second chances, or forgiveness, or reprieve.

Nursing home

The people in the ceiling
were explaining something
important but unclear.
I was on my way home, you said,
but I wound up back here.

Appointment at the cancer clinic

She thought she ought to wear a dress
the way she used to do for Mass:
white cotton gloves, a little straw hat,
girl-sized handbag with a metal clasp
she liked to fiddle with, snip and snap.
She had business to transact; pictures
of angels with devotions on the back;
a nickel for the collection basket;
in case of embarrassment, a Kleenex
Pocket Pack. On the back of the pew
there was a latch where, if she were a man,
she'd hang her hat. Light freckled her hands
through the raffia brim; her thoughts
stayed hidden; the strap was bothersome
under her chin. She swung her feet, couldn't
relax; her mother whispered, *Ants in your pants.*
In the presence of martyrs she didn't dare laugh.
She thought then of sacrifice, penitence, shame,
and slow ways of dying, perfected by saints.

Social inventory, midcentury

Returned servicemen who bought their houses for ten thousand
    dollars, mortgaged.
The widow whose beautiful husband had survived the war and
    then, abruptly, died.
The sisters who lived together so that one, infirm, could be cared
    for by the other two.
The only Jewish family.
The three francophone households.
The Polish family who bought the house of the couple who
    moved back to England.
The man who disowned his daughter when she married a Jamaican.
His wife, who gave their daughter's fairy tale books away, across
    the back fence, to a blonde girl.
The woman with velvet armchairs who painted in oils in
    the afternoon.
Her husband, who sold their house because she wanted
    a downtown apartment.
The same who, discovering his wife's fear of heights, bought
    their old house back again.
The musical family, with a croquet set and the biggest lawn.
The last family to allow a television in the house.
The women who played bridge.
The woman who vowed never to learn bridge, thus avoiding
    the conversation of women who played bridge.
The same, who disliked bridge or other women but sewed
    expertly and altered her neighbours' hems.
The women who never learned to drive.

The woman, the one who sewed and did not play bridge, who
    drove the others to Friday afternoon bowling.
The preschoolers who loved the bowling alley and the car wash.
The woman who had been in a sanatorium for tuberculosis.
Her husband, his model trains, and two smelly spaniels, Sparky
    and Jinx.
The ladies who made pinwheel sandwiches for the CWL with
    store-boughten bread sliced horizontally.
The children who said *boughten* until the day it sounded strange.
The woman with a glass eye whose husband was the alderman.
The man who had thought of becoming a priest, and almost no
    one knew.
The man who had thought of becoming a priest, and a lot of
    people knew.
The stillborn babies spoken of in secret, or never.
The boy whose parents didn't know he was bullied at school.
His friend, reader of fairy tales, who also had no clue but sat with
    him on summer evenings to imagine the end of the world.
The family whose eldest son was run over by a truck and
    survived.
The family whose youngest boy went to jail.
The postman whose son would heal by the laying-on of hands.
The boy, not the bullied one, who would marry the girl across
    the street.
The girl, not the clueless one, who would marry him.

Rue Sainte-Catherine, December

Waltzing her slowly
through revolving glass,
he's rhyming off the list
of things they need to buy
and holding her
like the biggest parcel
of the day so far.
I'd worry that she'll drop it,
that toy in her hand,
red rider on a horse,
jogging behind his shoulder
like an afterthought,
but I happen to know
the vestigial monkey-grip,
palmar and plantar
tree-dweller's clench,
lets go at six months—
which means a toddler's grasp
is intention, not reflex.

In other words,
she knows enough already
to hang on to what she's got.

Foshan market, October 13, 2011

In twenty ways,
Yue Yue
was reduced
to a simulacrum
of herself:
a light thump,
hesitation,
rear-wheel rocking,
brutal chance,
someone else's problem,
crime,
negligence,
Peng Yu effect,
rag doll,
rag,
red leggings,
figure pooling into ground,
rain on metal roofs,
closed-circuit evidence,
double take,
defensive glance,
steering clear,
stepping wide, or,
most bizarrely, walking close,
another small vibration under tires.

When the scrap picker found her,
she raised her left arm.
Oh darling, oh darling,
you were there still,
you were gone.

Sinus arrhythmia, pediatric

Sometimes even now
I sit beside her in the dark
powerless and amazed
that some dreaming thought
or heave of breath—
parasympathetic,
hypersynchronized—
connects beyond my reach
to her thrifty heart.

Science be damned.
How will I ever
take for granted
how daringly she paddles
on the waves within—
sensible,
sensitive,
saving beats
or quickening
as needed?

Afterbirth

When you were settled, safe,
the midwives, like grocers,
held up for admiration
the rich and weighty mass,
cradled in its shining sac
programmed, they explained,
for readiness, hence rupture.
A marvel, this on-demand,
single-use organ, first shared,
then spent, your time-travel map,
which they laid out and read,
tracing the corded vessels,
flecks of chalky sediment,
the flat mark, somehow familiar,
matched by a wound
that now softly bled.

It came to me later,
the still footprint,
smooth scar on dark water,
left by whales submerging—
a thing I learned with your mother
when she was a girl
and we took the Bay Bulls tour,
trying our luck to see them breaching.
The one that surprised us

rose so close to the boat
we reckoned it had followed us
all the while, inquisitive,
claiming space,
a little dangerous.

From here on in,
when I think of such days
before yours, I'll see you
swimming alongside,
a canny shadow
biding your time,
clenching your nuchal hand,
preparing to crest into salty air,
make landfall in our grateful arms.

Oh baby, grand girl,
for how many ages
have we been leaning
against the rail, gazing
over blue-grey waters,
waiting for you always,
already, to arrive.

LOSS LESSONS

Non sequitur

The day you called me up to quit,
the solstice was a blue exhaust
around the flame of winter.
We were deep into talk when
I caught a reflection of buffy wings
and looked out for a mourning dove
landing on snow. Whatever
you were saying then, my thoughts
trailed off to false migrations,
weather going wrong,
the seasons' sinister approximations,
and what it means to feel so soothed, so satisfied,
by the feeding of birds that are plain and industrious
and the local irruptions of redpolls or juncos.

And there it was: a kestrel
perched against argent,
brilliant, implausible,
sharply regardant
for seed-fattened mice
and the sparrows I'd lured.
An ancient pose, then volant.
I saw my mistake,
my delayed recognition,
in the colour above his wings.
What took my breath, to be honest,
wasn't the beauty of the bird

so much as the odds
against seeing it again.

Too strange a thing to mention
in the middle of an argument.
But I've been wondering ever since
if this, the smallest of the falcons,
was your totem, or mine.

This kind of speculation is mainly what I miss,
so I'm asking you now, if you're reading this.

Slant

Last we spoke, we sat in the yard of that hopeless duplex
I shared with my boyfriend. We plucked seed stalks from grass;
I showed you the vegetable patch, turned by a neighbour
with a gas-powered tiller when I asked to borrow a spade.
All that exhaust and noise and amendment of the soil, and still
I couldn't grow a decent root. I described my difficulties;
you said certain paths (faith, and marriage) aren't improved
by tangents of critique. Your skeptical phase over, those articles
of doubt written to an elder still unanswered, except by you
and further study of Mrs. Eddy. You took me once
to a Wednesday meeting. The crossless nave, embracing pews,
struck me as apostate, American, vaguely creepy,
but I admired how you asked, without leading, whether
I'd found the testimony convincing. Well no, not really—
not much in life holds up as proof, and I think you agreed.
But when a young man told me how, catching his hand
carelessly with a blade, he saw light pouring from his palm,
whereupon the wound was sealed, I found no reason to disbelieve,
aside from the fact that miracles never happened to me.

Another friend's story: long day at a jobsite raising cladding
to a roof. He found a way to move the metal quicker
and it all went south, sheets cascading like cards in a waterfall
with no dealer's hand to catch them. By grace or chance
no one was severed from the earth, but a guy he knew
at a sawmill in BC, dragged by a glove-buckle to a blade,
was a hair from his maker by the time a buddy leapt to the brake.

He rose, a crazed Lazarus, threw down his gloves, a *tabernac*;
went home to Saint-Clin-Clin, never came back.

If you were here now, gentle scientist, in my revised backyard,
an old field I've been watching for years now, filling in,
I'd want to ask how readiness for death fits with your belief.
I've been having, lately, strange experiences. If you consider
all nature immaterial, you might dismiss this instance: after rain,
a yellow bird fanning under leaves (the green shade sweet,
the spray of drops more radiant than any glass in old cathedrals),
stretched lyre-like and opened its beak as if proclaiming
a perfected earth, which I would just then have been satisfied
to leave. No illusion, as it struck me, no shadow of the real,
but as good as it will get for me: a soft blow landing like plain fact,
the way a barn door, unlatched by wind, swings abruptly into light.

War stories

Tallied against
your inheritance of grief,
what could it count for,
the sunny empathy
of someone like me,
whose kin have carried
a dumb-luck charm
for centuries? No exile,
famine, bombs, or burning;
no fodder for the Great War
or losses to the Spanish Flu;
two brothers in the Second
made it through. One ditched
his plane in the Irish Sea.
In broad daylight
he floated on a wing,
awaiting rescue.

One day the trees went mystical

You loved the dense mess
of the city: iron bridges,
water towers, shop-window puns,
publishers' remainder tables,
all-day-breakfast counters.

We spoke of good and evil
and the language between.
You were wracked by history.
I think I did apologize
for my remote acquaintance
with the facts. Looking back,
I'm not sure why you let me talk.

One day the trees
went mystical
and I said I felt it too
without admitting
But not as much as you.

They were maples, golden.
Sparrows shook the leaves
the way the first drops
of heavy rain
tell you it's time
to run for cover.

Biographical fallacy

The yearly card arrives:
your enviable script
sends lovelovelove and
a wonderful year.
No news, as usual.
I'm not even clear
on the names
of your children.
Hey you.
Unmedicated poet.
Every line
not only true
but gorgeous.
We drank coffee
and sweet liqueurs.
Stripped wallpaper
from our sad
apartments.
Got terrified
listening
to Prokofiev.
Never read
the same books.
Compared notes
endlessly
regardless.

Fish science

I took you for
the bare-armed boy
of childhood
who taught me
to thread worms
without flinching.
That boy was rude
but knowledgeable.
I read his taciturnity
as he muttered
one or two facts
about the habits of fish
as a kind of tenderness
toward the world
(by which I mean
an understanding).
Such was the peculiar
romanticism
of little girls
in those days—
to think men
were the masters
of science
and therefore
of love.

Remembrance Day

Passing the old neighbourhood. My father,
veteran, forgets the date, frets we're late
for his appointment. A small parade
swings out ahead, halting traffic
at the stone gates. I step out of the car
to stand and wait, look to those gathered
for old acquaintance. It's good to see
you there with a gentle-seeming man—
years enough since your husband
walked, weather-blinded, off the earth.

The local councillor, legionnaires, wreathe
the repaired memorial, speak to the occasion,
say a prayer, quote the buffed inscription:
Praise can add nothing to their gallant worth.

And Main Street breathes an awkward pause
in the minutes before our minutes are up:
horn-tap in the line of cars; cellphone
marimba; a sudden flare, like a stage effect,
of sunshine. It must be normal at such rites
to feel so restlessly alive, but also shamed
by squandering. Have we spoken even once
since the funeral? But to come forward now,
wave hello, would announce the wrong time,
as if offering that same basket of fruit at your door

while you calmly drew me inside, explaining
not how it happened or what the searchers found,
but the days of waiting, the life-raft voice
of the warden on the phone, making dread
almost tolerable by the strength
of his concern, until news arrived
in an unmarked car, plain clothes.
A tricky kindness, to slip such loss
into an as-if-ordinary day, when
you'd braced yourself so carefully
for death turned out in uniform.

Marco Polo

When I was housebound, ill,
commotion announced you
like the knife grinder's bell,
Dickie Dee chimes, the tinkling
of camels: children, wagon,
skipping rope, dog, strung together
in your sidewalk caravan,
bearing fruit from distant gardens
(kumquat, persimmon, lychee—
Ever had one? Like orgasm, you said),
a cargo of novelties, sweet plum pastries,
tales of family, theories of art.
On your views of a darkening world
I tried to sprinkle salt.

Funny, how my risky habit
of pouring it straight from the box
prompted your gift: an assortment
of salt-shakers, thrift-store rescues
wrapped like Christmas ornaments
in old news.

Looking for logic, I shuffled them
on a shelf. Cow, pig, chicken.
Chicken, egg. Egg, eggplant.
Potato, tomato. Cluster of grapes.
Twinned silos, corn-coloured,

from Sunny Saskatchewan
were the only set. No
Tweedledum and Tweedledee,
black cat and yellow dog,
left and right mittens,
Santa and the Missus,
but the way such duos
tend to wind up:
missing a sidekick
at the end of the match.

ASSISI VARIATIONS

The wolf explains

The arrow snapped in my shoulder.
It itches now, stinks, and I cannot reach.
You might pity me, at least—as he did,
thinking me gaunt from scarcity
when this untongued wound
makes me too feverish to hunt.
Do not blame, he said, *a starving animal.*
He called me brother, set down between us
dry bread. How brave they thought him,
parleying with the infamous *lupo di Gubbio,*
child killer, crossing two sticks as if
to baffle me. Bewildered little man,
blind to the old injuries from snares
I've been robbing all my life.

To clarify: the child's disappearance
had little to do with me. The path is steep.
Girls stagger up with their bloody bundles
and throw them over. The women said,
The river swallowed the child. An unfortunate
account, since I'm the one who eats.
But all I did was watch from the thicket
while he picked stones with his stubby hands,
his sandals untied. An odd gait, clumsy.
How should I know why, when one shoe
fell, I stepped forward, as if with a dog's
mind, to retrieve?

The father justifies himself

All I know is he stole from me,
made an ass of himself
before the magistrate,
disrobed in the village square,
standing like a poor jack
with his pitiful attributes
hanging like giblets
under that filthy hair-shirt,
and now he is begging for stones.

He hasn't been right in the head
since he was thrown
into that hole in Perugia.

He used to be such a happy boy
with his fine wardrobe
and foreign poetry.

The sultan recollects

How do I recall him?
Threadbare, unkempt;
a gaze that guttered
like a flame.
He gestured, babbled,
brimmed with tears.
By this we understood
he'd come to preach.

It was the sixteenth month
of the siege.

When I arrived from Cairo
they were battering the chain tower,
building mangonels, stealing cattle.
They advanced with eighty ships,
raining stones; masts snapped
under the weight of armour.
We poured fire from the walls;
they quenched it with acid and gravel.
Then, Paderborn's floating fortress,
cloaked in hides, unwieldy in the rising Nile;
ingenious, the revolving ladder
by which they gained the tower
and then unchained the river.

News of my father's death
came to me from Acre.

We built ramparts, scuttled ships,
harassed with rocks and arrows,
robbed them of sleep. Our raid
near Būrah failed. Lost to water
and the blade, a thousand heads
hurled back at us like stones.

They dredged the blue canal.
The same brought stormwater,
filling their tents with fish.
They fasted, prayed, repaired
a bulwark with the drowned
and horses slaughtered
for this purpose.

In their camp, pestilence;
in mine, conspiracy.
I was obliged to flee
until my brother came.
By then, we were surrounded.

I offered Jerusalem,
compensation,
a thirty-year peace.

They preferred to skirmish,
to starve, to siege.
They bedevilled us
with their machines.
At Fāriskūr we feigned retreat,
rounded, killed four thousand Franks.

I offered terms.
The flood plain was dry;
there was no grain
within the city walls.
Again, the fanatics stalled.
We tried all means until
an empty watchtower
betrayed the truth.
They entered the famished city,
looted, took slaves and women,
baptized children as they died.

Dogs gnawed on corpses. The living,
three of eighty thousand, lay beside.

For eighteen months they squabbled
and debauched while I built a new city
at al-Manṣūrah. I raised my offer.
For Dumyāṭ: Jerusalem, Sidon,
Tiberias, holdings in Syria.

But now their craving was for all of Egypt.

I trusted time. The river
and my brothers' armies
gathered strength.

Finally, from Fāriskūr,
three hundred ships,
many thousands of men
intent on Cairo, herded
by their own rabble
into a bottleneck of land.

We tightened the snare.
Then we opened the dykes.

They surrendered
for dry ground,
pomegranates,
bread.

I was a builder before then:
dams, schools, improvements
to the citadel, the dome
of the mausoleum. Uncounted,
the stones we knocked down
in advance of our enemies: palaces,
defences, the walls of Jerusalem.

Yet here you come to reminisce
about your little man of the book
as if I might remember nothing else.

Once or twice, perhaps, I wondered
what happened to him since.

He declined my gifts; accepted food.
I lent him the key to my prayer room.

An embroideress reflects

Punto Assisi, it's called, derived from
more than one ancient technique,
but not, as some vendors might imply,
the gentle Clare's invention,
nothing to do with her oh-so-spiritual boyfriend,
not a replica of an altar cloth she made,
but an opportunity seized by a women's guild
to build a cottage industry
on the holy reputation of this place.
The motifs, too, a pastiche of dates.
This one I'm stitching now, the griffin,
symbol of Perugia, his first enemy and captor,
muddies the history, don't you think?

No doubt Saint Clare would approve
the abstinent technique: the voided emblem,
white on red ground, the dark outline
of thread containing so cleanly
the exhausted space of love.

NOTES

January 1971

A record for the highest snowfall in Ottawa, Ontario, was set in the winter of 1970–71. It was snowfort heaven.

Strontium-90

The Baby Tooth Survey was initiated in St. Louis, Missouri, in 1958 by scientists, health professionals, and members of the public concerned about the effects of radioactive fallout from nuclear test blasts. Some 300,000 teeth were collected and sent for analysis to detect strontium-90, an isotope with an affinity for bone. The results helped convince US president John F. Kennedy to sign the Test Ban Treaty of 1963.

Trinitite

One of the names given to the glassy substance formed when desert sand and other materials were fused by the plutonium bomb detonated at the Trinity test site near Alamagordo, New Mexico, on July 16, 1945. *New York Times* science reporter William L. Laurence (1888–1977) was embedded with the test bomb team in the late stages of the Manhattan Project. He witnessed the Trinity test on the ground and, by air, the bombing of Nagasaki. His gee-whiz reporting, for which he won a Pulitzer Prize, participated in the effort to persuade the public that victims in Japan died from the blast and resulting fires only, and not from radiation. The phrases in the second stanza are borrowed from his reporting on September 26, 1945. After witnessing the Trinity blast, Kenneth T. Bainbridge (1904–1996), the test director, said, "Now we are all sons of bitches." The phrases "lake of jade" and "splashy star" were used by *Time* on September 17, 1945 to describe the crater.

Near Los Alamos
LANL is the Los Alamos National Laboratory, established in 1943 to support the Manhattan Project. Often pronounced "lannel."

Foshan market, October 13, 2011
On this date two-year-old Wang Yue was run over by a van in the Foshan market in Guangdong province, China. At least eighteen pedestrians passed her without stopping to help; during that time she was run over by a second vehicle. Little Yue Yue, as she was called, died of her injuries several days later. The Peng Yu effect refers to a 2006 case in Nanjing in which an injured woman brought legal action against a bystander who came to her assistance.

Afterbirth
Nuchal pertains to the nape of the neck; a nuchal hand or fist refers to an infant's hand held close to the neck or face during birth.

The wolf explains
lupo di Gubbio: One of the legends of Francis of Assisi (Giovanni di
Pietro di Bernardone, c. 1181–1226) concerns the taming of a wolf
that terrorized the Umbrian town of Gubbio.

The father justifies himself
"begging for stones": for the restoration of the church of San
Damiano.

"right in the head": Modern biographers of St. Francis, who was
the son of a wealthy silk merchant, surmise that he suffered from
post-traumatic stress disorder as a result of his battle experience
against the Perugians and a related year-long imprisonment.

The sultan recollects
The city of Dumyāṭ (Damietta), downriver from Cairo in the
Egyptian Nile delta, was besieged from 1218 until 1221 during the
Fifth Crusade and defended by the viceroy, then sultan, al-Ma-
lik al-Kāmil (d. 635/1238). The city's fortifications included three
encircling walls, a moat, twenty-eight towers, and Burj as-Silsi-
lah, a tower that stood opposite the city on an island in the Nile.
Between the tower and the city wall was an iron chain, or chains,
that controlled the passage of boats. During a lull in the conflict,
Francis visited the sultan in his camp outside the city. Whether his
main objective was to achieve martyrdom, the sultan's conversion
to Christianity, or an end to hostilities is a matter of speculation.
The encounter appears not to be recorded in Muslim chronicles
of the period. My "variation" is influenced by, among other texts:

Farhan Mujahid Chak, "Islam and the Myth of the Other: The Noble Colloquy between St. Francis of Assisi and Sultan al-Malik al-Kāmil," *Muslim World* 109 (January/April 2019): 126–43; Fareed Z. Munir and Jason Welle, "Foreword," *Muslim World* 109 (January/April 2019): 3–13; James M. Powell, *Anatomy of a Crusade 1213–1221* (Philadelphia: University of Pennsylvania Press; 1986); and Thomas C. Van Cleve, "The Fifth Crusade," in *A History of the Crusades*, Vol. 2, ed. R. L. Wolff and H. W. Hazard (Madison: University of Wisconsin Press; 1969), 366–428.

An embroideress reflects

"Punto Assisi": a form of counted-thread embroidery in which the main motif, left blank or "voided," is outlined with dark thread against a coloured ground.

THANKS

My unending thanks to Barry Dempster for his generous and inspiring editorial guidance. My gratitude also to Alayna Munce for her hawk-eyed and astute edits, to Marijke Friesen for her beautiful design, and to everyone at Brick Books for so ably sustaining the work of making poems. My thanks to fellow poet Suzanne Nussey for her friendship, readings, and encouragement. To Lawrence, winter sweeper: my love and inarticulate gratitude for your apparently indefatigable support. "Near Los Alamos" and "Orion Sweeping" are for you. "Afterbirth" is for Sage, and for Emily, whose wise heart continues to astound me. "Farmyard behaviour" is for WM.

Earlier versions of some of these poems have appeared in *Ars Medica*, *Arc Poetry Magazine*, *The Best Canadian Poetry in English*, *CV2*, *The Malahat Review*, *The New Quarterly*, *Ottawater*, *Prairie Fire*, and *The Winnipeg Review*. I am grateful to their editors and staff for giving time, care, and space to my work, and to the adjudicators and sponsors of *Arc*'s Poem of the Year contest and Diana Brebner Prize, the Banff Centre Bliss Carmen Poetry Award (*Prairie Fire*), the Nick Blatchford Occasional Verse Contest (*TNQ*), and the editors of the *Best Canadian Poetry in English* series.

I live in Wollaston Township, Ontario, within Michi Saagiig ancestral territory and the lands delineated by the Rideau Purchase—Treaty 27 (1819) and Treaty 27¼ (1822)—and adjacent to the watershed of the Algonquins of Ontario Land Claim. I respectfully acknowledge the past and present importance of this region to many Anishinaabeg, Huron-Wendat, and Haudenosaunee peoples. I am grateful for my sojourn here and all that the land teaches me.

Born and raised in Ottawa, Anne Marie Todkill has lived in Toronto, Kingston, and Edinburgh. She spent many years as an editor but has since embarked, with her husband, on a experiment in conservation on a mixed-habitat acreage in "the country north of Belleville," where she writes poetry and prose, watches turtle nests, and thinks about human and natural histories. *Orion Sweeping* is her first book.